EXTREME POKÉMON

The Ultimate Guide for Poké-Fanatics!

by MICHAEL TEITELBAUM

SCHOLASTIC INC.

New York Toronto London Auckland Sydney

Mexico City New Delhi Hong Kong

For Adam and Ari, for introducing me to the monsters; Sean and Kerri, for their Poké-expertise; and Parker, my movie buddy.

Special thanks to Maria Barbo for her editorial guidance and support, to Chris at 4Kids for all the right names, and to Randi for the chance.

ISBN 0-439-19401-6

12 11 10 9 8 7 6 5 4 3 2 1   0 1 2 3 4 5 6/0

Printed in the U.S.A.
First Scholastic printing, July 2000

CONTENTS

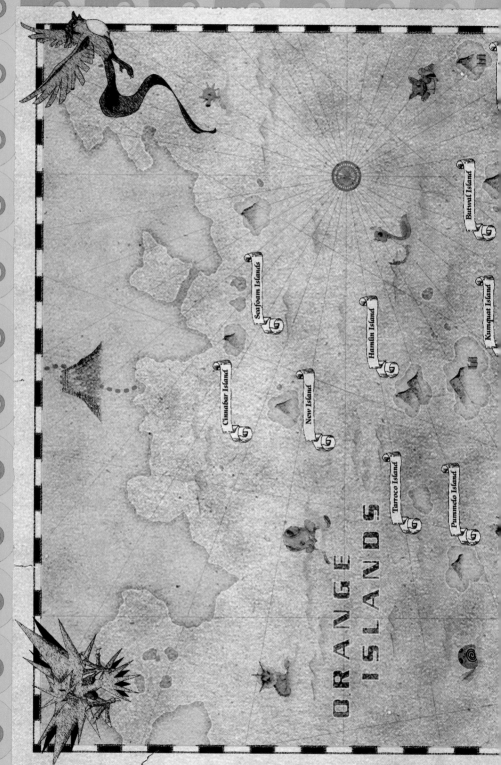

Bitival Island

Seafoam Islands

Kumquat Island

Hamlin Island

Cinnabar Island

New Island

Tarroco Island

Pummelo Island

ORANGE ISLANDS

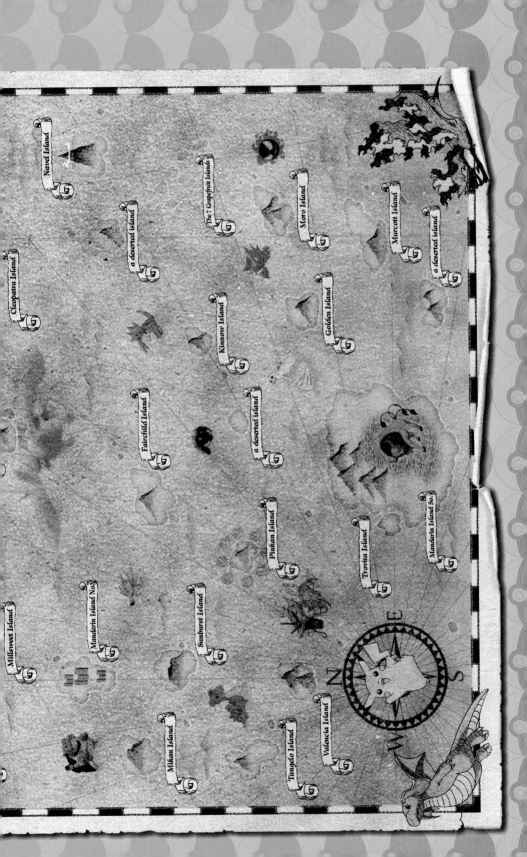

CHAPTER

1

WHAT IS POKéMON ALL ABOUT?

What is Pokémon all about?

Sure, everyone knows the Poké-phenomenon started as a popular video game. Millions of Pokémon lovers everywhere have battled, collected, traded, and trained their way to becoming Pokémon Masters.

But what is Pokémon all about?

Yes, it's an animated television show, following the adventures of Ash Ketchum as he journeys toward his goal of becoming Pokémon Master, while making new friends and enemies, competing in Pokémon matches, and catching wild Pokémon.

But what is Pokémon all about?

Yes, it's collectible trading cards! It's hit movies, and a best-selling series of books.

• •

But what is Pokémon all about?

Glad you asked.

Most of all — Pokémon is about friendship. It's caring about the Pokémon you collect and respecting each Pokémon's uniqueness and personality. It's about recognizing your Pokémon's strengths and weaknesses, as you train them, battle with them, or just plain love them. No two people are exactly the same. Well, no two Pokémon are either. Caring, collecting, training, trading, even watching (the TV show and movies) are the ways that Pokémon fans and trainers get to connect with the sometimes lovable, sometimes fierce, always surprising creatures.

Pokémon is also about teamwork! Working together with your Pokémon as a team is the key to winning battles and keeping them strong and healthy.

So now it's time to leap into the Pokémon world — you've probably got one foot in there already, don't you! This guide brings you up-to-date on the adventures of Ash, Misty, Brock, and Tracey, as well as those bumbling baddies, Jessie and James of Team Rocket. There's a recap of Ash's first Pokémon League Tournament on the Indigo Plateau. You'll learn about the mysterious Orange Islands and the Orange Crew. Plus, you'll meet the newest Pokémon, challenge yourself with trivia, quizzes, and lots more!

What is Pokémon all about?

Just the coolest collection of characters ever!

Pokémon fans — GO!

CHAPTER 2

WHAT'S UP WITH ASH?

Ash Ketchum's goal is clear. He wants to be the world's greatest Pokémon Master. Ash knows that to reach this goal he has to teach his Pokémon well, and he also has to learn a lot from them.

With his faithful friend and first Pokémon, Pikachu, by his side, Ash journeys far and wide on his quest. Along the way he's made some friends: Misty, the Cerulean City Gym Leader; Brock, the Pewter City Gym Leader; and Tracey Sketchit, a Pokémon watcher and artist. Ash also caught Pokémon like Bulbasaur, Charmander, Caterpie, Primeape, Krabby, Muk, Tauros, Pidgeotto, Snorlax, and Lapras.

Ash earned eight badges by battling eight Gym Leaders in order to qualify to compete in the Pokémon League Tournament on the Indigo Plateau. After picking up his Earth Badge (his eighth) by defeating Team Rocket's Jessie and James in the Viridian City Gym, Ash moved onto the Indigo Plateau where he realized a dream — to compete in the Pokémon League Tournament.

Ash made it past the first four rounds (Water Field, Rock Field, Ice Field, Grass Field), and battled into the fifth round of competition in Indigo Stadium (see chapter 3 for more details). Although he didn't win the tournament (he came in sixteenth), Ash made a new friend (Richie) and learned from his mistakes.

Following that tournament, Ash returned home to Pallet Town for a brief rest before taking off on an errand for his good friend and mentor, Professor Oak. Ash traveled to the distant Orange Islands to pick up a mysterious Gold and Silver (GS) Poké Ball from Professor Oak's colleague, Professor Ivy. On the way, Ash's Pidgeotto evolved into a Pidgeot!

After successfully getting the GS Poké Ball from Professor Ivy, Ash learned that the Orange Islands had their own Pokémon League. He immediately set off to win the four badges required to compete in the Orange Islands Pokémon League Tournament.

Ash's travels in the Orange Islands continue as he battles Gym Leaders, earns new badges, captures new Pokémon — including Snorlax and Lapras — and sees many wondrous sights, such as a surfing Pikachu (named Puka)!

ASH'S INDIGO LEAGUE BADGES

Gym		Gym Leader		Badge
Pewter City Gym		Brock and his dad, Flint		Boulder Badge
Cerulean City Gym		Misty and her sisters		Cascade Badge
Vermilion City Gym		Lt. Surge		Thunder Badge
Saffron City Gym		Sabrina		Marsh Badge
Celadon City Gym		Erika		Rainbow Badge
Fuchsia City Gym		Koga		Soul Badge
Cinnabar Island Gym		Blaine		Volcano Badge
Viridian City Gym		Jessie and James		Earth Badge

CHAPTER 3

SHOWDOWN ON THE INDIGO PLATEAU— THE POKéMON LEAGUE TOURNAMENT

The following articles are ripped from the sports pages of the *Pokémon Times*:

POKéMON TIMES SPORTS NEWS

INDIGO TOURNAMENT OPENS! FIRST-ROUND ACTION BEGINS!

It only happens once a year, and I'm not talking about Christmas! The annual Pokémon League Tournament on the Indigo Plateau opened today with the usual fanfare. The sacred flame, believed to have been lit by Moltres, the legendary bird Pokémon, burned brightly above Indigo Stadium.

Following the colorful opening ceremonies, first round action began. Ash Ketchum of Pallet Town battled Mandy the Astounding on the Water Field. As you may know, a trainer can't battle in the main Indigo Stadium until he or she has won battles on the first four fields — Water, Rock, Ice, and Grass.

Each trainer was limited to three Pokémon. Ash led off with Krabby, Mandy with Exeggutor, and this year's pulse-pounding Pokémon action was underway!

POKéMON TIMES SPORTS NEWS

Exeggutor started with a Psywave. Krabby dove underwater and hardened.

Then Exeggutor's Barrage Attack pulled up a wall of water, preventing Ash from recalling his Krabby! Krabby countered with a Vicegrip, grabbing Exeggutor's leaves, stopping it from using other attacks. Following up with a Leer, then a Stomp, Krabby won the round, then immediately evolved into Kingler!

In a bold move, Ash left his newly evolved Kingler in the match. Mandy called on Seadra, a Water Pokémon. Kingler's Bubble Attack caught Seadra off guard. Kingler followed with a Crabhammer that clinched the second round for Ash.

In a last chance effort, Mandy called on Golbat, a Poison and Flying Pokémon, turning this final round into a sea-and-sky contest! Golbat swooped toward Kingler, striking with Razor Wind, followed by a Mega Drain. But just when things looked bleak for Ash, Kingler turned the tables with a Hyper Beam that took Golbat out.

Ash Ketchum, the rookie, won the first tournament battle of his career. A great start, but tomorrow brings another round!

POKéMON TIMES SPORTS NEWS

RUMBLE ON THE ROCK FIELD ROUND TWO

Ash Ketchum, victorious in his first-ever Pokémon League battle yesterday, took the Rock Field today in second-round action. Ash faced off against the Red trainer, who chose Nidorino, a Poison-type Pokémon known for its power attacks. Ash chose Squirtle, hoping its hard shell could withstand a blow from Nidorino's nasty horn.

Nidorino immediately took the offensive opening with a Tackle Attack. Squirtle used its Withdraw Attack to avoid the blow, then Ash called for Squirtle to counter with a Water Gun that really caught Nidorino off guard. Momentarily gaining the upper hand, Ash took full advantage by ordering Squirtle's Skull Bash. This on-target attack was more than Nidorino could handle. Squirtle did the job, and Ash claimed another victory, moving into the third round on the Ice Field. More tomorrow!

POKéMON TIMES SPORTS NEWS

CHILLY COMPETITION! ICE TIME IN ROUND THREE!

The third round of competition here on the Indigo Plateau got off to a frosty start on the Ice Field. Ash Ketchum battled a trainer known only as Pebbleman. Ash called on his recently evolved Kingler to put the deep freeze on Pebbleman's Cloyster.

Kingler led with a Crabhammer Attack, but Cloyster withdrew into its hard shell. Ash's face told the story as he tensely watched his Kingler maintain the Crabhammer. "I was worried that Kingler might be getting worn out," Ash told reporters after the match. "I was afraid I might have to switch to another Pokémon. But Kingler really hung in there."

Indeed it did! Keeping its Crabhammer firmly in place, Kingler eventually wore out Cloyster, earning yet another victory for Ash Ketchum!

POKéMON TIMES SPORTS NEWS

GRASSY FIELD OF DREAMS— ROUND FOUR!

Pallet Town's Ash Ketchum took to the Grass Field in round four of the Pokémon League Tournament. This is the final stepping stone for trainers before they can compete in the main stadium here on the Indigo Plateau.

Ash's round-four opponent was Jeanette, who opened with Beedrill. Ash countered with Bulbasaur and the attacks came fast and furious. Beedrill began with a Tackle Attack. Bulbasaur used its Razor Leaf. Beedrill countered with a Twineedle followed immediately by a Poison Sting. Ash struck hard with Bulbasaur's Leech Seed, which ultimately drained all of Beedrill's energy, giving the first part of this battle to Ash.

Jeanette followed with Scyther, unleashing Slash, Swift, and Double Team Attacks. Ash's Bulbasaur

POKéMON TIMES SPORTS NEWS

used a Vine Whip, which took advantage of Scyther's weak defense. It tied up the dangerous Bug Pokémon.

Ash stuck with Bulbasaur as Jeanette chose a Bellsprout for her final Pokémon. Ash called for Bulbasaur's Tackle Attack, but Bellsprout used its ability to turn Bulbasaur's power against it for the victory.

Giving Bulbasaur a much needed rest, Ash brought in Pikachu, whose Thundershock was rendered harmless when Bellsprout directed the electricity into the ground. Bellsprout's Axe Kick knocked Pikachu right out of the competition. Now,

that's a well-trained Pokémon!

Round four all came down to this: Ash's Muk against Jeanette's Bellsprout. The energy from Bellsprout's powerful Axe Kick was absorbed by Muk's big squishy body. Muk's bulky Body Slam knocked Bellsprout out, and gave victory in round four to Ash!

One side note, Ash's fellow Pallet Town trainer and biggest rival, Gary Oak, was defeated in round four action today by Melissa on the Rock Field. Her Golem beat Gary's Nidoking, leaving Ash Ketchum as the only Pallet Town trainer moving on to round five.

POKéMON TIMES SPORTS NEWS

INDIGO STADIUM AT LAST— ROUND FIVE!

Emotions ran high for Pallet Town's Ash Ketchum as he took the field in Indigo Stadium for round five. His mom, and his mentor, Professor Oak, were among the cheering throng rooting him on. Ash was thrilled at the chance to compete in the main stadium at last. But his opponent was a new friend, Richie. The two friends promised to give each other the battle of a lifetime, and they did not disappoint the capacity crowd.

Ash showed up late, but when the battle finally began it was a good one. Ash started with Squirtle, Richie chose Butterfree, whose Sleep Powder Attack put Squirtle right to sleep.

Ash chose Pikachu next, and its Thundershock knocked Butterfree out of the contest. Richie sent in Charmander, who attacked Pikachu with a Flamethrower followed by a Tackle. The pooped-out Pikachu was

POKéMON TIMES SPORTS NEWS

overwhelmed and lost the battle.

It was time for drastic measures. Ash released Charizard, who was notorious for not obeying him! Richie recalled his Charmander and sent out Sparky, his Pikachu.

And that, folks, is when it happened. Ash's Charizard took a nap! Right in the middle of the most important battle of Ash's life. Sparky picked up an easy victory for Richie, who took the match, knocking Ash from the competition here in the fifth round.

Richie was defeated in the sixth round by a trainer named Assunta, and Ash placed in the top sixteen of the overall competition. Both trainers made this an action-packed, thrill-a-minute tournament for the crowd here on the Indigo Plateau. Fans can't wait to see them in action again next year!

CHAPTER

4

TROPICAL TOUR BOOK—THE POKéMON TRAINER'S GUIDE TO THE ORANGE ISLANDS

Every Pokémon trainer worth his or her Poké Ball knows about the Indigo League. It's all about gyms, Gym Leaders, and badges. But it's a whole different world in the large group of islands collectively known as the Orange Islands — or the Orange Archipelago.

This tropical paradise consists of beautiful white sand beaches lined with palm trees. The Orange Islands also have their own Pokémon League with their own unique set of rules. Even the Pokémon look different!

So, if you're thinking of taking a trip to the Orange Islands, be sure to bring this handy guidebook (and lots of sunscreen). Take a look!

ORANGE ISLANDS LEAGUE RULES

In order for a Pokémon trainer to compete in the Orange League, he or she must battle and defeat the four Orange Islands Gym Leaders, known as the "Orange Crew." As in the Indigo League, you earn a badge when you defeat a Gym Leader. It takes four badges to enter the Orange League Tournament — Coral-Eye Badge, Sea Ruby Badge, Spikeshell Badge, and Jade Star Badge.

TRAINER and POKéMON —
TWO HEARTS THAT BEAT AS ONE

Friendship, trust, loyalty, teamwork, and working toward a single goal — that's what the Orange Islands League is all about. As one of its greatest Pokémon Masters, Prima, said:

"In the Orange League, the most important thing is that the trainer and his or her Pokémon be of a single heart. As trainers compete side-by-side with their Pokémon, they strengthen their friendship and learn about their Pokémon's individual abilities."

In the Orange Islands gyms, the contest between Gym Leader and challenging trainer consists of much more than simply having their Pokémon battle each other. Cleverness contests, skill tests, and challenges of how well a trainer's Pokémon have been trained are what make up the competition for badges.

THE NINE HABITS OF HIGHLY EFFECTIVE POKéMON TRAINERS

As you travel from island to island on your Orange Islands Pokémon journey, you'll meet Pokémon trainers and Masters willing to offer advice. A wise trainer keeps his or her eyes and mind open. Listen, learn, and consider this advice as you continue on your personal journey to become a Pokémon Master.

Pokémon Master Prima:

• "A Pokémon trainer is only as good as his or her Pokémon."

• "Trainers' badges are simply gifts from their Pokémon, showing how much their Pokémon care for them."

• "Every trainer must learn that losing is an important part of becoming a Pokémon Master. Defeat makes you wiser — if you learn from your mistakes and trust your Pokémon."

• "Listen to your Pokémon. Understand them and feel what is in their hearts."

Trovita Island Gym Leader, Rudy:

• "You can improve your Pokémon's attack abilities by training them in something completely unrelated to that attack. Dancing, for example."

Mikan Island Gym Leader, Cissy:

● "In the Orange Islands gyms we do a lot more than just have our Pokémon battle each other. Pokémon use their skills to meet challenges."

Navel Island Gym Leader, Danny:

● "Even if you can't be totally prepared for the surprises life has in store, always try to plan where you are going and what you'll need before you begin."

World's greatest Pokémon expert, Professor Oak:

● "To aid a Pokémon in distress you must start by knowing what that Pokémon needs and wants. Pokémon have wills just as you do. Don't try to bend that will to suit you."

Pokémon trainer, Ash Ketchum:

● "To get along with a Pokémon, the most important thing you have to keep in mind is that Pokémon's personality. Every Pokémon is different from every other Pokémon, just like all people are different."

ORANGE LEAGUE GYMS

Here's a rundown of the need-to-know info on the Orange Crew. For more details, check out the sections in this guide on each.

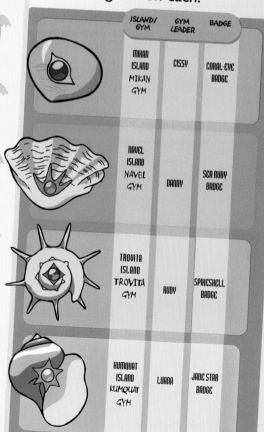

ISLAND/ GYM	GYM LEADER	BADGE
MIKAN ISLAND MIKAN GYM	CISSY	CORAL-EYE BADGE
NAVEL ISLAND NAVEL GYM	DANNY	SEA RUBY BADGE
TROVITA ISLAND TROVITA GYM	RUDY	SPIKESHELL BADGE
KUMQUAT ISLAND KUMQUAT GYM	LUANA	JADE STAR BADGE

POKÉMON CENTERS

Not all the islands in the Orange Archipelago have Pokémon Centers. Only major islands like Valencia Island, Tangelo Island, Murcott Island, and Mikan Island have their own centers. For the rest, Nurse Joy (yes, there's a Nurse Joy in the Orange Islands, too!) paddles around in her boat with Chansey by her side, doing what she can to help sick and injured Pokémon.

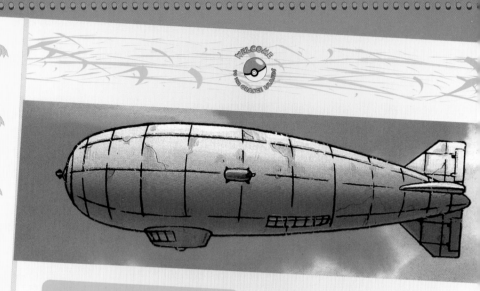

HOW TO GET THERE

The fastest way for tourists to reach the Orange Islands is by blimp or hot air balloon. A trip from the mainland usually takes less than a day. But be careful. If the hot air balloon looks like Meowth of Team Rocket, do yourself a favor — take a boat!

The trip by boat takes a few days over some rough seas. Of course, if you're a Pokémon trainer and you happen to have a large flying Pokémon like a Pidgeot, hop on its back and hang on! Before you know it, you'll be splashing in the crystal clear ocean, or competing in the Orange Islands Pokémon League!

THE ISLANDS

VALENCIA ISLAND

If you're a Pokémon trainer you should stop by the Valencia Island Pokémon Center to make sure your Pokémon are fit and ready before attempting to compete against any of the Orange Crew. Nurse Joy — the second cousin of the sister-in-law of the Nurse Joy in Saffron City — will be happy to help.

Professor Ivy bred and raised all the Pokémon on the island. Now she and her assistants, Faith, Hope, Charity, and Brock (Ash's friend), study, observe, and train mostly Water Pokémon, like Gyarados, which live in the bay right next to Professor Ivy's lab. She is also studying how Pokémon adapt to their environment. You'll see familiar Pokémon that look just slightly different because they live in the Orange Islands' tropical climate. For example, Raticate, which are usually brown, are red! The Weepinbell are orange instead of yellow, and Paras are covered with orange triangles instead of yellow dots!

Valencia Island is a great place to start your journey through the Orange Islands.

PROFESSOR IVY'S LAB

HOT SPOT: Be sure to visit Professor Ivy's research laboratory, located on Bayview Road, not far from the Pokémon Center. It's a great learning experience for all Pokémon trainers.

TANGELO ISLAND

If you're a tourist, this is the island for you. If you're a Pokémon trainer, you'll have to put up with lots of tourists! Why? Because Tangelo Island is home to Pokémon Park, the world's first Pokémon theme park, run by the Tangelo Island Chamber of Commerce. Huge cruise ships dock here, and hundreds of camera-toting tourists fill the park. If you've got Pokémon with you, don't be surprised if the tourists want you and your Pokémon to pose for a picture!

If you're a serious trainer, pass through the park as quickly as possible and begin your training. Tangelo Island is where most trainers who want to take on the Orange Crew get their start.

MIKAN ISLAND

On Mikan Island you'll encounter your first Gym Leader and your first chance to earn an Orange Islands badge. But it won't be easy. Cissy, the Mikan Island Gym Leader, is one of the toughest trainers in the Orange Crew.

It's here you will first see how the Orange Islands are different from other places.

I see seashells on the seashore — well, sure — all the Orange Islands badges are made from seashells!

THE LAPRAS LOWDOWN

In the Orange Islands, Ash saved a Lapras from some young trainers who were mistreating it. He caught the Lapras and used it as a boat, riding on its back from island to island.

- Lapras is a combination Water and Ice Type Pokémon.
- Its main attacks are Water Gun, Body Slam, and Ice Beam. In fact, Lapras's Ice Beam helped Ash earn his Coral-Eye Badge on Mikan Island by freezing the water during the deciding Pokémon Wave Ride contest. It slid home to victory!
- Lapras is sweet, gentle, and kind. Its good-natured personality and generosity (after all, it did become Ash's own private "boat"!) made finding this nearly extinct Pokémon a high point of Ash's Orange Islands journey.

Rather than battling Pokémon, Cissy will present you with several challenges. "In my gym," Cissy likes to say, "Pokémon compete like athletes, head-to-head, one-on-one."

Cissy will ask you to choose Pokémon from your team with the best Water Gun Attack. Then you and your Water Pokémon will face three challenges: 1) a head-to-head competition with Cissy's Seadra to see which Pokémon can knock over the most cans with its Water Gun; 2) a test of speed and accuracy in which your Water Pokémon has to hit a moving target with its Water Gun; 3) a quick-draw contest to see which Pokémon — yours or Cissy's Seadra — can fire its Water Gun Attack fastest and hit a moving target.

If you can keep up with Cissy in these tests of skill, the winner will be determined by a Pokémon Wave Ride. You'll have to pick another Pokémon to race and surf against Cissy, with you on its back! If you triumph you'll walk away with the Coral-Eye Badge — your first step on the road to competing in the Orange Islands League!

MANDARIN ISLAND

Mandarin Island is a giant city of skyscrapers floating in the ocean. It's the most built-up of the Orange Islands, and an interesting change of pace. Mandarin is a center for theater and business, and life there moves at a faster pace than on the more tropical islands in the group.

But beware! With big cities come big city problems. Team Rocket baddies

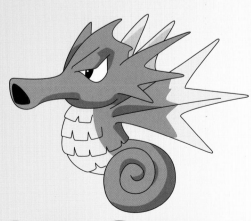

Butch and Cassidy have been known to hit Mandarin Island with their Pokémon-stealing plots. Most recently, they ran Drowzee's Hypnosis Attack through an antenna to try to gain control of all the Pokémon on the island. Luckily, Ash Ketchum and his friends thwarted the plan.

SUNBURST ISLAND

The most unique Pokémon in all the Orange Islands can be found on Sunburst Island — the rare and beautiful crystal Onix. It is literally a living Onix made of glass. Artists on the island say that they draw

HOT SPOT: Sunburst Island is famous for its many crystal and glass shops. Lots of artists live and work here, making fine glass sculptures of Pokémon. People come to the island from all over the world to buy these beautiful figurines.

THE SNORLAX FAX

inspiration from this mysterious, sparkling Pokémon.
The crystal Onix lives deep
in a cave and is rarely seen.
But if you ask a sculptor
named Mateo, he may lead
you to the cave for a
glimpse of a truly awesome
Pokémon.

Citrus SOS! Ash helped save all the grapefruit on the Grapefruit Islands, when a Snorlax threatened to eat the entire crop! Ash then caught the Snorlax, adding another Pokémon to his team.

• Snorlax is a Normal Type Pokémon.

• Snorlax is the heaviest Pokémon ever found (1,014 pounds).

• It loves to eat and sleep. In fact, Snorlax is so lazy it will lie down in the middle of a road or a lake! It eats up to 900 pounds of food a day (so you under-stand why those grapefuit were in danger!).

• Its main attacks are Head Butt, Rest, and Body Slam — for obvious reasons!

• Did you know Snorlax could swim? It uses the butterfly stroke to get from island to island.

Like some kids, Pokémon don't really care how nutritious their food is. They like food that tastes good (hey, who doesn't?)!

PINKAN ISLAND

Pinkan Island is strictly off limits to visitors! It's a protected Pokémon preserve, patrolled by Officer Jenny (who else?). And it's surrounded by huge whirlpools powerful enough to pull even the biggest boats underwater. The island is also bordered by giant cliffs on all sides.

What you're missing by not seeing the island is pink Pokémon. That's right. Pink Rhydon, pink Nidoking, even pink Pidgey! This is why Jenny and the other park rangers want the outside world kept away. The Pokémon are pink because they grew up eating Pinkanberries, small pink berries that only grow on the trees covering this island.

The biggest fear the rangers have is that poachers will invade the island to steal the pink Pokémon. But fear not, Officer Jenny is on the job keeping these Pokémon in the pink!

NAVEL ISLAND

A journey to Navel Island will put you face-to-face with the second member of the Orange Crew — Danny, the Navel Island Gym Leader.

It's not easy to take on Danny and earn your Sea Ruby Badge. All Navel Gym challengers must climb to the top of a snowy mountain on their own — without any help from their Pokémon — just to prove their worthiness! If you make it to the top, you and your Pokémon must then face three contests of skill: 1) turning hot water into ice; 2) carving the ice into the shape of a sled: 3) racing down the mountain on the ice sled your Pokémon have carved.

If you and your Pokémon win two out of three of these contests you will earn the Sea Ruby Badge, the second of the four Orange Islands badges.

GRAPEFRUIT ISLANDS

It's easy to guess how these islands got their name. This chain of seven islands is covered with groves and groves of huge, juicy, delicious grapefruit. A grower named Ruby is in charge of the groves, which she fiercely protects from thieves.

THE POOP ON PIDGEOT

Look out Ash! It's a Spearow and Fearow attack! Ash's Pidgeotto comes to the rescue and saves Ash from the attack, at the start of the young trainer's journey to the Orange Islands. Then suddenly, Pidgeotto evolves into a Pidgeot!

• Pidgeot can fly at twice the speed of sound at an altitude of nearly one mile.

• Pidgeot is a combination Normal and Flying Type Pokémon.

• Its main attacks are Gust, Whirlwind, and Wing.

• It is brave and loyal and will fight fiercely for its trainer.

What is the secret to growing such huge grapefruit? In Ruby's own words: "It takes a lot of work and more than a little bit of love. Every winter we wrap the trees with straw to protect them from the cold. We trim them and weed them. When the warm weather comes and the trees are in blossom, we gather Butterfree from the neighboring islands to pollinate the trees so they can produce fruit."

But Ruby must always be on the lookout for the grapefruit-snarfing Snorlax, who once almost ate her entire crop!

Buh-bye, Brock!?! You bet! Brock was so impressed by the Orange Islands, specifically Professor Ivy's research (not to mention Professor Ivy herself!), that he decided to leave his companions, Ash and Misty. He stayed on Valencia Island with Professor Ivy, to help her in her study of the native Pokémon.

The Grapefruit Islands are quite a sight to see (and taste, if you're lucky), even if the visit doesn't improve your chances of getting to compete in the Orange League!

TROVITA ISLAND

A short ferry ride away from the bustling urban energy of Mandarin Island lies Trovita Island, home of the Trovita Gym. There, you'll compete against Rudy, the Gym Leader, to earn the third of your Orange Islands badges.

MIME'S THE WORD

Who says a lot without ever speaking? Why it's Mr. Mime! Ash's mom took a Mr. Mime home from a circus where it was being treated harshly. It now helps her with household chores!
- Mr. Mime is a Psychic Type Pokémon.
- Its main attacks are Confusion and Barrier.
- Mr. Mime uses body movements to make real walls appear. It hates to be interrupted while miming, and if it gets angry, it will slap you around with its huge hands.

Rudy will put you through two tests: 1) the attack test in which your Pokémon must use an attack to knock down targets that Rudy flings into the air; and 2) the type test, which is a series of Pokémon battles pitting Pokémon of the same type against each other — your Electric against his Electric, your Grass against his Grass, and so on.

If you can handle these matches successfully, the Spikeshell Badge will be yours.

SOUTHERN ISLANDS

This grouping of islands at the southern tip of the Orange Archipelago is home to some rare Pokémon such as Farfetch'd, a wild duck Pokémon that can be seen here in large flocks. There

It's a major award! Ash received a Certificate of Distinguished Achievement from Officer Jenny for his help in stopping Team Rocket's Butch and Cassidy from capturing all the Pokémon on Mandarin Island.

have also been sightings of the super rare trio of legendary birds — Articuno, Zapdos, and Moltres!

VENONAT VIRTUES

Hunting for a hard-to-find Pokémon? No problem if you've got a Venonat. Just show it a picture of the Pokémon you're looking for. Its radar ability will guide the way as it does so often for Pokémon watcher Tracey Sketchit in his search for unusual Pokémon to draw and study.

• Venonat is a combination Bug and Poison Type Pokémon.
• Its main attacks are Tackle and Disable.
• Venonat moves among the shadows, loves to eat insects, and sometimes flies a bit too close to bright lights at night.

Rare and beautiful! While in the Southern Islands, Tracey spotted the rare trio of legendary birds — Articuno, Zapdos, and Moltres! A definite highlight of his journey!

Trainers who have successfully earned all four Orange League badges earn the chance to compete for a trophy in the Orange League championships.

MURCOTT ISLAND

This thickly wooded island is home to many Bug-type Pokémon including Beedrill, Caterpie, and Scyther. Misty would just hate it here! It also has a Pokémon Center.

KUMQUAT ISLAND

Here you will have the chance to earn your fourth and final badge — the Jade Star Badge — competing against Luana. When you land on Kumquat Island head straight for the newly renovated Kumquat Hotel. The hotel manager is the fourth member of the Orange Crew. She'll let you stay at the hotel free of charge while you get ready to face off.

The Kumquat Gym looks more like a stadium than a Pokémon Gym. Battle here

Tracey captured a Scyther on Murcott Island. The Scyther had been leader of its insectlike swarm until it lost a leadership battle to a younger Scyther. Then it was forced to leave the swarm. Scyther, a combination Bug and Flying Type Pokémon, uses its razor-sharp wings and ninja-fast reflexes to make its Swords Dance Attack almost unstoppable!

is unique, too. A double battle takes place with each trainer using two Pokémon at once. Victory at this gym is decided when either of the two Pokémon is unable to continue fighting. You'll face some tough challengers here. Luana uses a powerful Alakazam and Marowak combination. Make sure you choose two Pokémon that get along well. They'll have to work together if you want to earn the Jade Star Badge and go on to compete for the Orange League Winner's Cup.

GOLDUCK GOSSIP

The evolved form of Psyduck, Golduck is a strong, powerful fighter. Surprisingly for a Water Pokémon, Golduck fights equally well in water and on land. Misty thought her Psyduck had evolved to battle and beat fellow Water Type trainer Marina. But it was a wild Golduck who liked to help out female trainers.

- Its main attacks are Scratch, Tail Whip, and Disable.
- Golduck is sometimes mistaken for a legendary Japanese sea monster named Kappa.

All aboard! The Pokémon Showboat travels around the Orange Islands. It's a floating theater in which humans provide the voices for Pokémon who act out dramatic scenes.

TRACEY

CHAPTER 5

THE NEW KID IN TOWN – TRACEY SKETCHIT

When Brock decided to stay with Professor Ivy on Valencia Island, Ash and Misty were sad. They knew they would miss their friend. But almost as soon as they arrived on

Tangelo Island they met Tracey Sketchit — an excellent companion and a good friend.

Tracey is a Pokémon watcher and a Pokémon artist (get it — Sketch it?). He loves to observe Pokémon in the wild. Then he draws detailed pictures of them. When he first met Ash and Misty he could tell that a Spearow wasn't getting enough vitamins, a Beedrill's coloring was off, and a Hitmonchan wasn't getting enough exercise, just by taking a quick look at the Pokémon. He also told Ash that Pikachu's electric sacks were in great shape (phew — good news!).

Ash and Misty were very impressed by Tracey's Pokémon smarts. Tracey explained that Pokémon watchers go looking for all kinds of Pokémon so they can observe and study (and in his case, sketch) their characteristics and abilities. Pokémon watchers even search for new and rare Pokémon.

Tracey's hero is Professor Oak. "Every watcher knows Professor Oak is one of the greatest Pokémon experts on the whole entire planet!" Tracey explained. When he learned that Ash and Misty were friends with Professor Oak, he asked if he could join them in their travels, hoping to meet his hero one day.

Ash and Misty agreed, and a new friendship was formed.

TRACEY'S POKéMON

Marill, a Water Type Pokémon, with fantastic hearing and a floating tail that helps it swim.

Scyther, a Bug Type Pokémon. Scyther has razor-sharp wings and the spirit of a warrior.

Venonat, a Bug and Poison Type Pokémon with excellent radar ability.

TRACEY'S TIPS FOR POKéMON WATCHERS

A good Pokémon watcher can predict a Pokémon's next attack by the way it moves. If you follow these two rules the Pokémon won't know you're watching, and you'll get a closer look.

The two basic rules of Pokémon watching are:
1) Stay downwind of the Pokémon you are approaching so it can't smell you.
2) Make your breathing match the Pokémon's breathing as you get close to it, so it can't hear you.

CHAPTER
6

EVERYTHING I NEED TO KNOW, I LEARNED FROM WATCHING POKéMON
POKéMON WORDS OF WISDOM

Ash learns quite a bit about Pokémon, but also about life, on his journey to become a Pokémon Master. Here are some of the important things his experiences have taught him:

CARING IS MORE IMPORTANT THAN WINNING

While battling Blaine, the Cinnabar Island Gym Leader, to win his Volcano Badge, Ash chose Pikachu to fight against Magmar. Magmar, the spitfire Pokémon, wasn't hurt by Pikachu's high voltage Thundershocks. But Pikachu was almost scorched by Magmar's volcanic Flamethrower Attack. The loyal and brave Pikachu didn't want to stop battling and let Ash down.

Pikachu teetered on the edge of a boiling lava pit inches away from the burning hot liquid. Magmar set up for another Flamethrower Attack. This next blast would have surely sent Pikachu tumbling into the pit.

"Your little Pikachu doesn't know when to give up," Blaine said.

"Forget it, Pikachu," Ash called. "Return!" Then he looked at Blaine and added, "I quit. No badge is worth losing Pikachu!"

"I congratulate you for making a wise decision, Ash," Blaine said. "If you had been foolish enough to continue the match, you would have been disqualified as a Pokémon trainer. You showed me that you understand that caring about your Pokémon is more important than winning."

THE QUALITY OF YOUR FRIENDSHIPS IS MORE IMPORTANT THAN THE NUMBER OF FRIENDS YOU HAVE

Ash returned home to Pallet Town to train for the Pokémon League Tournament. When Ash went to visit Professor Oak, he found his rival Gary in the lab as well.

Professor Oak looked over both trainers' Pokédexes. He learned that although Ash had seen more Pokémon than Gary during their travels, Gary had captured many more Pokémon than Ash — over two hundred, compared to only a few for Ash!

"I capture them first and ask questions later," Gary boasted. "You can never have too many Pokémon. That's my motto!"

"You may have a lot of Pokémon, Gary," Ash said. "But I bet they're not your friends."

"Friends?" Gary scoffed. "Ha! Who cares if you're friends with your Pokémon, as long as you've got a lot!"

"Having lots of Pokémon isn't what's important," Ash explained. "It's what you teach them, and what you learn from them that counts. The most important thing about being a good Pokémon trainer is to be a good friend to your Pokémon."

HOLD ON TO YOUR DREAMS. IT'S NEVER TOO LATE FOR THEM TO COME TRUE

On Seafoam Island, Ash met a surfer named Victor who told him the story of the Humungadunga — the biggest wave of all time!

Forty years earlier a surfer named Jan had ridden the Humungadunga all the way up to the top of a tall rock. He planted a flag on the top of the rock, where it still stands to this day. Since that time, surfers from all over the world came to the island to ride the Humungadunga wave and try to do what Jan did. No one had ever succeeded.

Victor always dreamed of matching Jan's achievement. He first tried forty years ago, but failed. His disappointment was so great that he stopped surfing altogether. Then, twenty years ago a Pikachu named Puka came to Victor from the sea.

"I can't explain how it happened, but from that day on, Puka and I have never been apart," Victor said. "Once I found Puka, I learned to love surfing all over again."

Puka loved surfing, too. Victor said that his Pokémon could actually feel the waves in its body. Victor and Puka tried again to surf the Humungadunga wave to the top of the rock, but again Victor failed.

"Since then, Puka and I have teamed up and conquered every kind of wave you can imagine," Victor explained to Ash. "There's just one left — Humungadunga!"

"You and Puka can do it!" Ash replied. "This time I know you're going to beat it!"

Victor held onto his dream. Victor and Puka rode the big wave and planted Victor's flag on top of the tall rock, with Ash cheering him on the whole way.

ALWAYS BELIEVE IN YOURSELF

In the Xanadu flower nursery in Pallet Town, Ash met a Pokémon trainer and gardener named Florinda. Her family had owned the nursery for many years. Now she was responsibile for running the nursery, but she didn't think she was up to the job.

"I'm a big failure at raising Pokémon," Florinda said. "I can't even train my Gloom properly. And if I can't do that, how will I ever run a huge nursery? I guess the reason my Gloom hasn't grown strong is that I haven't given it enough love."

But when Team Rocket attacked the nursery, trying to steal Ash's Pikachu, Florinda was forced to use her Gloom in battle.

"Go, Gloom!" Florinda commanded. "Solar Beam Attack!"

Gloom's attack blew Team Rocket right out of the nursery.

Even Professor Oak said that this was the most impressive Solar Beam Attack he'd ever seen.

"But how did Gloom get so strong?" Florinda wondered.

"Because of the love and care you gave it," Ash explained. "Your Gloom was getting stronger all the time. All you needed to do was believe in yourself!"

STEALING FROM ONE PERSON IS LIKE STEALING FROM EVERYONE

Ash met a young Pokémon trainer on the road from Pallet Town to the Indigo Plateau and the Pokémon League Tournament. Otoshi challenged Ash to a Pokémon battle. The winner had to give up all his badges. This meant that the loser couldn't compete in the Pokémon League Tournament!

Ash accepted the challenge and beat Otoshi. That's when he learned that Otoshi had no badges to give up. Ash was angry at first, then he listened to Otoshi's story.

"I fell into a trap and my badges were stolen," Otoshi explained. He was close to tears. "I worked so hard to get those eight badges. Now all my struggles and sacrifices were for nothing."

Ash had to make a difficult decision. If he helped Otoshi get his badges back he might be late for the start of Pokémon League competition.

"We have to get your badges back," Ash said. "I worked hard to earn my badges, too. I know how I'd feel if somebody stole them. Stealing from one trainer is like stealing from all trainers. Now let's go get those badges back!"

WHAT A PERSON LOOKS LIKE IS NOT IMPORTANT, IT'S WHAT A PERSON DOES THAT IS IMPORTANT

As Ash arrived for the Pokémon League Tournament at the Indigo Plateau, he ran into a trainer carrying the sacred tournament torch. It was made from the flames of Moltres, the legendary bird of fire.

"I'd like to carry that torch," Ash said.

"Only participants in the Pokémon League can carry the torch," Officer Jenny explained.

"But I'm here to participate in the Pokémon League," Ash replied, showing off his badges.

"I don't know," said Officer Jenny suspiciously. "You look like a trouble-maker."

"Why not let him have a chance," an old man with a long white beard spoke up. "Don't judge the young man by his looks."

"Who are you?" Ash asked. "You look like Santa Claus!"

"This is President Goodshow, head of the Pokémon League torch committee," Officer Jenny explained.

"Well, he doesn't look like a president," Ash said.

"That's right!" President Goodshow exclaimed. "This young man may look like a troublemaker, and I may look like Santa Claus, but what a person looks like is not important. It's what a person does that is important. I say, let him carry the torch!"

And Ash did. All the way to Indigo Stadium!

LEARN FROM YOUR MISTAKES, DON'T STRESS ABOUT THEM

Ash's friend Richie defeated him at the Indigo Plateau Pokémon League Tournament. Then Richie was defeated in the next round.

After his loss, Ash sat around feeling sorry for himself and moping about losing. Misty and Brock tried to cheer him up, but Ash refused their kindness and even their company. He went for a walk to be by himself, but he ran into Richie.

"If I knew how hard the Pokémon League was going to be I'd have trained twice as hard as I did," Ash said, still moping.

"Losing isn't so bad," Richie said. "Now I know what mistakes not to make next time. I'll be a better trainer for it."

Richie doesn't feel sorry for himself, Ash thought. *He just wants to do better and learn from his mistakes.*

"Let's make a promise, Richie," Ash said. "To keep working hard and become Pokémon Masters no matter what!"

"You've got a deal!" Richie replied, and the two friends shook hands on it.

MISTY

CHAPTER

7

CLEARING UP THE FACTS
ABOUT MISTY

Misty, a trainer who loves Water Pokémon, left behind her responsibilities as a Cerulean City Gym Leader to join Ash on his Pokémon journey. At first, Misty traveled with Ash because he had borrowed and wrecked her bicycle. She planned to hang around with him until he could pay her back. But as they had new adventures, met new Pokémon, and visited exciting and amazing places, Misty began developing her own talents as a Water Pokémon trainer.

She got to participate in the Princess Festival, a special holiday in which women and girls rule, and men and boys have to do whatever they say. What a great chance to boss Ash around!

Misty competed in the Queen of the Princess Festival contest — a series of Pokémon battles. She beat Jessie of Team Rocket in the finals, using her Psyduck's psychic power. Misty was named Princess Festival Queen, winning a set of beautiful Pokémon Princess dolls, something she had wished for since she was a little girl. During her travels with Ash and Brock, Misty returned home to Cerulean City when her Horsea became sick. A long swim in the Cerulean City Gym's pool was just what Horsea needed to get well.

Misty traveled with Ash and Brock to the Orange Islands. There she met Professor Ivy, a researcher with a large collection of Water Pokémon. Misty also met Marina, a trainer who shared her love of Water Pokémon and helped Misty find her missing Psyduck.

Misty's journey continues, as she develops her talent as a Pokémon trainer, with her beloved Togepi at her side. Her other Pokémon are Starmie, Staryu, Goldeen, Psyduck, and Horsea.

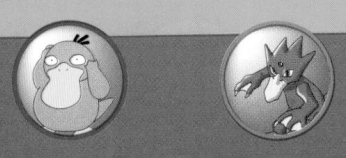

51

CHAPTER 8

POKÉMON TYPES

Pokémon types let you know the characteristics of each Pokémon and what attacks it will use in battle. Here's a quick type chart to help you train and battle your Pokémon.

FIRE

#04 CHARMANDER™

#59 ARCANINE™

#05 CHARMELEON™

#77 PONYTA™

#37 VULPIX™

#78 RAPIDASH™

#38 NINETALES™

#126 MAGMAR™

#58 GROWLITHE™

#136 FLAREON™

POISON

#23 EKANS™

#33 NIDORINO™

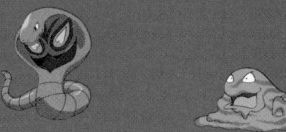

#24 ARBOK™

#88 GRIMER™

#29 NIDORAN™ ♀

#89 MUK™

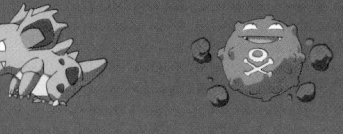

#30 NIDORINA™

#109 KOFFING™

#32 NIDORAN™ ♂

#110 WEEZING™

FIGHTING

#56 MANKEY™

#57 PRIMEAPE™

#66 MACHOP™

#67 MACHOKE™

#68 MACHAMP™

#106 HITMONLEE™

#107 HITMONCHAN™

WATER

#07 SQUIRTLE™

#08 WARTORTLE™

#09 BLASTOISE™

#54 PSYDUCK™

#55 GOLDUCK™

#60 POLIWAG™

#61 POLIWHIRL™

#86 SEEL™

#90 SHELLDER™

#98 KRABBY™

#99 KINGLER™

#116 HORSEA™

#117 SEADRA™

#118 GOLDEEN™

#119 SEAKING™

#120 STARYU™

#129 MAGIKARP™

#134 VAPOREON™

MARILL™

DRAGON

#147 DRATINI™

#148 DRAGONAIR™

ELECTRIC

 #25 PIKACHU™

 #100 VOLTORB™

 #26 RAICHU™

#101 ELECTRODE™

#81 MAGNEMITE™

#125 ELECTABUZZ™

#82 MAGNETON™

 #135 JOLTEON™

PSYCHIC

#63 ABRA™

#97 HYPNO™

#64 KADABRA™

#122 MR. MIME™

#65 ALAKAZAM™

#150 MEWTWO™

#96 DROWZEE™

#151 MEW™

GROUND

 #27 SANDSHREW™

#50 DIGLETT™

 #104 CUBONE™

 #28 SANDSLASH™

 #51 DUGTRIO™

 #105 MAROWAK™

GRASS

 #114 TANGELA™

NORMAL

#19 RATTATA™

#39 JIGGLYPUFF™

#108 LICKITUNG™

#132 DITTO™

#20 RATICATE™

#40 WIGGLYTUFF™

#113 CHANSEY™

#133 EEVEE™

#35 CLEFAIRY™

#52 MEOWTH™

#115 KANGASKHAN™

#137 PORYGON™

#36 CLEFABLE™

#53 PERSIAN™

#128 TAUROS™

#143 SNORLAX™

BUG

#10 CATERPIE™

#11 METAPOD™

#127 PINSIR™

GRASS / POISON

#01 BULBASAUR™

#43 ODDISH™

#69 BELLSPROUT™

#02 IVYSAUR™

#44 GLOOM™

#70 WEEPINBELL™

#03 VENUSAUR™

#45 VILEPLUME™

#71 VICTREEBEL™

WATER / ICE

#87 DEWGONG™

#91 CLOYSTER™

#131 LAPRAS™

WATER / PSYCHIC

#79 SLOWPOKE™

#80 SLOWBRO™

#121 STARMIE™

BUG / POISON

#13 WEEDLE™

#14 KAKUNA™

#15 BEEDRILL™

#48 VENONAT™

#49 VENOMOTH™

ICE / PSYCHIC

#124 JYNX™

NORMAL/FLYING

#16 PIDGEY™

#22 FEAROW™

#17 PIDGEOTTO™

#83 FARFETCH'D™

#18 PIDGEOT™

#84 DODUO™

#21 SPEAROW™

#85 DODRIO™

GRASS/ PSYCHIC

#102 EXEGGCUTE™

#103 EXEGGUTOR™

ROCK/GROUND

#74 GEODUDE™

#76 GOLEM™

#75 GRAVELER™

#95 ONIX™

ROCK/WATER

#138 OMANYTE™

#140 KABUTO™

#139 OMASTAR™

#141 KABUTOPS™

GHOST/POISON

#92 GASTLY™

#93 HAUNTER™

#94 GENGAR™

EXTREME POKÉMON

FIRE/ FLYING

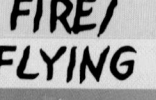

#06 CHARIZARD™

#146 MOLTRES™

POISON/ GROUND

#31 NIDOQUEEN™

#34 NIDOKING™

BUG/ FLYING

#12 BUTTERFREE™

#123 SCYTHER™

POISON/ FLYING

#41 ZUBAT™

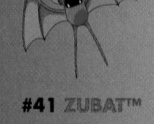

#42 GOLBAT™

BUG/ GRASS

#46 PARAS™

#47 PARASECT™

WATER/ POISON

#72 TENTACOOL™

#73 TENTACRUEL™

GROUND/ ROCK

#111 RHYHORN™

#112 RHYDON™

WATER/ FLYING

#130 GYARADOS™

WATER/ FIGHTING

#62 POLIWRATH™

DRAGON/ FLYING

#149 DRAGONITE™

ROCK/ FLYING

#142 AERODACTYL™

ICE/ FLYING

#144 ARTICUNO™

ELECTRIC/ FLYING

#145 ZAPDOS™

CHAPTER 9

YOUR POKéMON DICTIONARY
AN ALPHABETICAL GUIDE TO ALL THINGS POKé

Antidote — Cures a Pokémon that has been poisoned.

Archipelago — A group of islands, like the Orange Islands.

Awakening Potion — Wakes up a Pokémon that has been put to sleep.

Blizzard Attack — Used by Ice-Type Pokémon, like Jynx, to freeze an opponent.

Boulder Badge — An Indigo League badge won by defeating Brock, the Pewter City Gym Leader.

Bubble Attack — Used by Water Pokémon, like Squirtle, to slow down an enemy.

Bug Types — Pokémon that have the characteristics of insects. For example: Weedle, Beedrill, and Scyther.

Burn Heal — Soothes Pokémon that have been burned by fire attacks.

Calcium — Improves special Pokémon powers.

Carbos — Increases speed.

Cascade Badge — An Indigo League badge won by defeating Misty or her sisters, the Cerulean City Gym Leaders.

Celadon City — It has a Pokémon Center, a fully stocked department store, a game arcade, and a gym where you can earn your Rainbow Badge.

Cerulean City — Hometown of Misty (Gym Leader). It has a Pokémon Center, a PokéMart, a bike shop, a Pokémon trading post, and a gym where you can earn your Cascade Badge.

Cinnabar Island — In the middle of the sea, west of the Seafoam Islands, lies tiny Cinnabar Island. It's got a Pokémon Center, a PokéMart, a Pokémon lab where important Pokémon research is always being done, and a gym where you can earn your Volcano Badge.

Confusion Attack — Used by Psychic-Type Pokémon to disorient an opponent.

Coral-Eye Badge — An Orange League badge won by defeating Cissy, the Mikan Island Gym Leader.

Dome Fossil — If you bring this fossil to the scientists on Cinnabar Island, they'll turn it into a Kabuto.

Dragon Types — Pokémon that have the characteristics of large reptiles. There are only three known Dragon Pokémon: Dratini, Dragonair, and Dragonite.

Earth Badge — An Indigo League badge won by defeating Giovanni. He's the Viridian City Gym Leader and the head of Team Rocket.

Electric Types — Pokémon that have the ability to blast opponents with high voltage electricity. For example: Pikachu, Magnemite, and Electabuzz.

Elixer — Improves all of a Pokémon's abilities.

Fighting Types — Pokémon that specialize in hand-to-hand combat, martial arts, and boxing. For example: Primeape, Machop, and Hitmonchan.

Fire Spin Attack — Used by Fire-Type Pokémon, like Charizard, to burn enemies.

Fire Stone — Triggers evolution in certain Fire-Type Pokémon like Growlithe and Vulpix.

Fire Types — Pokémon that have the ability to scorch opponents with flaming attacks. For example: Charmander, Ninetales, and Magmar.

Flamethrower Attack — Used by Fire-Type Pokémon like Charizard and Magmar to burn an opponent.

Flying Types — Pokémon that can fly. For example: Pidgey, Spearow, and Aerodactyl.

Fuchsia City — This seaside town contains the Safari Zone, home to many rare and unique Pokémon. It also has a Pokémon Center, a PokéMart, and a gym where you can earn your Soul Badge.

Full Heal — Cures any condition ailing a Pokémon.

Ghost Types — Pokémon that can float through walls, make themselves invisible, and haunt old buildings and ships. There are only three known Ghost-Type Pokémon: Gastly, Haunter, and Gengar.

Grapefruit Islands — A group of islands in the Orange Islands. They are famous for growing huge, delicious grapefruit.

Grass Types — Pokémon that have plantlike characteristics. For example: Bulbasaur, Gloom, and Bellsprout.

Great Ball — Even more effective at catching Pokémon than a Poké Ball.

Ground Types — Pokémon that dig and live in the ground. For example: Sandshrew, Dugtrio, and Cubone.

GS Ball — A special Poké Ball that is gold on top and silver on bottom. It cannot be transported from one lab or Pokémon Center to another like regular Poké Balls. Scientists like Professor Ivy and Professor Oak are trying to figure out how to open the ball so they can learn more about it.

Helix Fossil — If you bring this fossil to the scientists on Cinnabar Island, they'll turn it into an Omanyte.

Hydro Pump Attack — Used by Water-Type Pokémon, like Squirtle, to blast an enemy with powerful jets of water.

Hypnosis Attack — Used by Psychic-Type Pokémon, like Drowzee, to put an opponent to sleep.

Ice Heal — Defrosts frozen Pokémon.

Ice Types — Pokémon that have the ability to freeze an opponent. There are no Pokémon who have Ice as their only type. But there are several Pokémon that have Ice as their secondary type. For example: Dewgong, Cloyster, and Lapras.

Indigo Plateau — Home of the annual Pokémon League Tournament.

Iron — Increases a Pokémon's defensive strength.

Jade Star Badge — An Orange League badge won by defeating Luana, the Kumquat Island Gym Leader.

Lavender Town — This tiny town is home to the Pokémon Tower, a place where dear, departed Pokémon are laid to rest. Devoted trainers attend memorial services in the tower for their beloved Pokémon. Rumor has it that the tower is haunted by evil spirits. You'll find a Pokémon Center and a PokéMart in town, as well.

Leaf Stone — Triggers evolution in certain Grass-Type Pokémon, like Exeggcute and Weepinbell.

Mandarin Island — An island in the Orange Islands. It contains giant skyscrapers, theaters, and businesses.

Marsh Badge — An Indigo League badge won by defeating Sabrina, the Saffron City Gym Leader.

Master Ball — This version of a Poké Ball will capture a Pokémon one hundred percent of the time. But you can only have one of them!

Mikan Island — An island in the Orange Islands. It contains a gym where you can earn your Coral-Eye Badge by defeating Cissy, the Gym Leader.

Moon Stone — Triggers evolution in certain Pokémon like Clefairy, Jigglypuff, Nidorina, and Nidorino.

Mt. Moon — Filled with twisting, turning caves, this mountain contains rare Pokémon fossils as well as lots of Paras, Geodude, Golem, Graveler, Clefairy, and Clefable. Watch out for Team Rocket! They often come here to steal the rare and valuable fossils.

Murcott Island — An island in the Orange Islands. It contains many kinds of Bug Pokémon.

Navel Island — An island in the Orange Islands. It contains a gym where you can earn your Sea Ruby Badge by defeating Danny, the Gym Leader.

Normal Types — Pokémon without any one particular thing in common. For example: Clefairy and Meowth. Many Normal-Type Pokémon have secondary types that better define their characteristics. For example : Farfetch'd (secondary type: Flying).

Old Amber — If you bring this fossil to the scientists on Cinnabar Island, they'll turn it into an Aerodactyl.

Orange Crew — The name given to the four Orange Island Gym leaders — Cissy, Danny, Rudy, and Luana.

Orange Islands — A group of islands out in the ocean, which have their own league of Pokémon Gyms, their own way of holding Pokémon competitions (stressing skills over battling), and different-looking Pokémon. Also known as the Orange Archipelago.

Pallet Town — Hometown of Ash Ketchum and Gary Oak. The starting point of many young trainers' journeys.

Paralyze Heal — Frees a Pokémon that can't move.

Pewter City — Hometown of Brock (Gym Leader). It's got a Pokémon Center, a PokéMart, a Science Museum with a collection of Pokémon fossils, and a gym where you can earn your Boulder Badge.

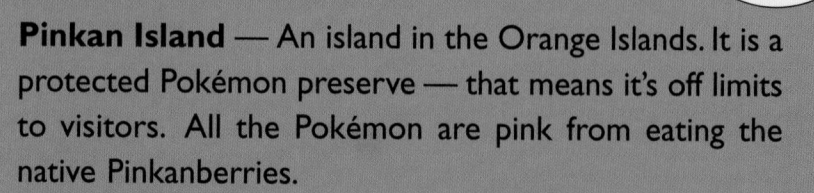

Pinkan Island — An island in the Orange Islands. It is a protected Pokémon preserve — that means it's off limits to visitors. All the Pokémon are pink from eating the native Pinkanberries.

Poison Gas — Attacks an opponent with toxic fumes.

Poison Types — Pokémon that have the ability to attack their opponents with toxic gas, poison stings, and sludge. For example: Nidoran, Grimer, and Ekans.

Poké Ball — Basic tool for catching wild Pokémon and carrying around all the Pokémon you catch. Press the button to release or call back your Pokémon.

Pokédex — A handheld computer containing info on all known Pokémon. It also stores new Pokémon data acquired by trainers and maintains a record of how many Pokémon a trainer has seen and caught.

Poké Flute — Wakes sleeping Pokémon.

Pokémopolis — A mythical city where Pokémon were worshiped as symbols of nature's power. It is believed that the city was buried by a giant storm.

Potion — Heals a Pokémon's wounds.

Professor Oak's Lab — In Pallet Town, home of the World's Greatest Pokémon Expert. This is where many trainers go to choose their first Pokémon: Squirtle, Bulbasaur, or Charmander.

Protein — Increases a Pokémon's attack strength.

Psybeam Attack — Used by Psychic Pokémon, like Kadabra and Alakazam, to confuse an opponent.

Psychic Types — Pokémon that attack opponents using powerful mental energy. For example: Drowzee, Alakazam, and Mr. Mime.

Rainbow Badge — An Indigo League badge won by defeating Erika, the Celadon City Gym Leader.

Rare Candy — Boosts a Pokémon's energy level — and tastes great!

Razor Leaf Attack — Used by Grass-Type Pokémon like Bulbasaur to slice through almost anything.

Revive — Wakes up Pokémon that have fainted.

Rock Types — Pokémon that are rough, hard, solid, and look like they are made of stone. For example: Geodude, Graveler, and Onix.

Route 1 — The road that leads north from Pallet Town to Viridian City.

Route 2 — The major path leading from Viridian City to Pewter City.

S.S. *Anne* — A Pokémon cruise ship docked at Vermilion City. Professional and amateur Pokémon trainers meet on board each year to ride this luxury liner and stage Pokémon battles.

Saffron City — The largest city in the land. It has a Pokémon Center, a PokéMart, the Silph Company head-quarters (run by Team Rocket), and two gyms! There's a regular Pokémon gym where you can earn your Marsh Badge by defeating Sabrina, the Gym Leader. There's also a Fighting Dojo Gym, for Fighting-Type Pokémon only. Defeat Karate Master in the Fighting Dojo Gym, and you'll get a Pokémon, either Hitmonlee or Hitmonchan.

Seafoam Islands — A group of islands off the coast of Fuchsia City. It's the home of many Water Pokémon.

Sea Ruby Badge — An Orange League badge won by defeating Danny, the Navel Island Gym Leader.

Silph Scope — Used to identify Ghost Pokémon in Lavender Town's Pokémon Tower.

Sing Attack — Used by Normal-Type Pokémon to put an opponent to sleep.

Smog Attack — Used by Poison-Type Pokémon like Koffing and Weezing to fill an area with poisonous smoke.

Soul Badge — An Indigo League badge won by defeating Koga, the Fuchsia City Gym Leader.

Southern Islands — A group of islands in the Orange Islands. They are home to some unique Pokémon such as Farfetch'd, a wild duck Pokémon, and the rare trio of legendary birds — Articuno, Zapdos, and Moltres!

Spikeshell Badge — An Orange League badge won by defeating Rudy, the Trovita Island Gym Leader.

Sunburst Island — An island in the Orange Islands. It contains many crystal and glass shops, where fine sculptures are made. It is also home to the rarely seen Crystal Onix.

Tangelo Island — An island in the Orange Islands. It contains Pokémon Park, the world's first Pokémon theme park.

Thunder Badge — An Indigo League badge won by defeating Lt. Surge, the Vermilion City Gym Leader.

Thundershock Attack — Used by Electric-Type Pokémon to strike an opponent with a high voltage blast of electricity.

Thunder Stone — Triggers evolution in certain Electric-Type Pokémon like Pikachu.

Trovita Island — An island in the Orange Islands. It contains a gym where you can earn your Spikeshell Badge by defeating Rudy, the Gym Leader.

Ultra Ball — One of the most effective tools to catch Pokémon.

Valencia Island — An island in the Orange Islands. It contains Professor Ivy's research laboratory.

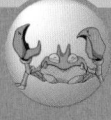    

Vermilion City — The Pokémon cruise ship S.S. *Anne* docks at this port city. It also has a Pokémon Center, a PokéMart, a Pokémon trading post, the headquarters of the Pokémon Fan Club, and a gym where you can earn your Thunder Badge.

Vine Whip Attack — Used by Grass-Type Pokémon to reach out from their backs and tie up an opponent with long plantlike tentacles.

Viridian City — A bigger city than Pallet Town. It has a Pokémon Center, a PokéMart, and a gym where you can battle Giovanni to earn your Earth Badge.

Viridian Forest — A lush, wooded nature preserve along the highway from Viridian City to Pewter City (Route 2). It's filled with wild Pokémon. Many trainers come here to catch wild Pokémon or challenge other trainers.

Volcano Badge — An Indigo League badge won by defeating Blaine, the Cinnabar Island Gym Leader.

Water Gun Attack — Used by Water-Type Pokémon, like Squirtle and Starmie, to fire a powerful stream of water at an opponent.

Water Stone — Triggers evolution in certain Water-Type Pokémon, like Shellder and Poliwhirl.

Water Types — Pokémon that live in or near lakes, rivers, oceans, or ponds and have the ability to blast opponents with jets of water. For example: Squirtle, Goldeen, and Staryu.

CHAPTER 10

BROCK AND ROLL!

Brock is an older and more experienced Pokémon trainer than Ash and Misty. He got his experience as the Pewter City Gym Leader, a job he held while raising his ten brothers and sisters.

When his father returned home to take care of the family, Brock hit the road with Ash and Misty. He was often the voice of reason in the trio, giving advice to the two young trainers who quickly became his friends.

Brock never wanted to use his Pokémon in competition. His goal is to become the world's greatest Pokémon breeder. He loves caring for Pokémon and learning all he can about them.

Brock went with Ash and Misty to the

Orange Islands to pick up a mysterious Poké Ball from Professor Oak's colleague, Professor Ivy. When the trio arrived at Professor Ivy's Lab on Valencia Island, Brock was blown away by the research the professor was doing about the effects of the environment on Pokémon.

Brock immediately went to work helping Professor Ivy. He fed stubborn Pokémon who wouldn't eat. He also swept the floor, washed the clothes, cooked the dinners, mopped, polished, and cleaned. In no time, he felt as if he had found a new home. Realizing that he could be of great help to Professor Ivy both as a researcher and a housekeeper, Brock decided to end his travels with Ash and Misty and stay at Professor Ivy's lab for a while.

His future as the world's greatest Pokémon breeder seems bright! Brock's own Pokémon include Geodude and Onix, plus Zubat and Vulpix.

TRIVIA

CHAPTER
11

ANSWERS TO ALL PUZZLES, RIDDLES, AND QUIZZES BEGIN ON PAGE 104

TRIVIA, FUN, AND ALL THAT COOL STUFF!

POKÉMON PERSONALITY QUIZ

WHICH POKÉMON ARE YOU MOST LIKE? WHICH ARE YOUR FRIENDS MOST LIKE? MATCH UP THE PEOPLE IN YOUR CLASS (YOUR TEACHER, TOO) TO THESE POKÉMON.

Alakazam™ — A super brain. A genius. Brilliant. High I.Q. Get the point? This Pokémon is really, really smart!

Bulbasaur™ — It can be cynical and complain a bit, but this Pokémon is loyal, loving, and determined.

Chansey™ — Although mysterious and a bit elusive, it will be a true friend and bring you lots of happiness.

(73)

Charizard™ — In a word, stubborn. Does what it likes, not what it's told!

Clefable™ — Very, very shy. Needs to be treated with lots of love and gentleness before it will trust anyone.

Clefairy™ — Kind, gentle, sweet, innocent, friendly, peaceful. A loving companion.

Ditto™ — A real follower. Mostly wants to do what everyone else is doing, and look like everyone else, too. Dresses like its friends, talks like its friends, acts like its friends.

Drowzee™ — A real sleepyhead. Will doze off anytime.

Ekans™ — Cunning and tricky. Trainers beware!

Gengar™ — A bully. Likes to scare people, then laugh at them when they get frightened.

Goldeen™ — Cool and classy. Really knows how to dress.

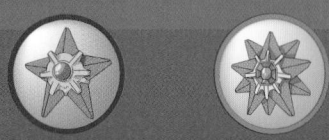

Grimer™ — A supreme slob! This Pokémon needs a bath! Can you say, "Piggy-Wiggy"?

Gyarados™ — Talk about a temper!

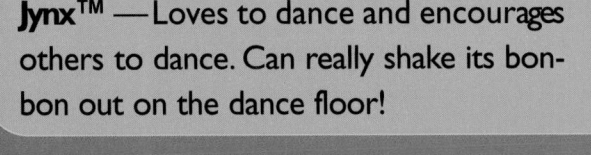

Jynx™ — Loves to dance and encourages others to dance. Can really shake its bonbon out on the dance floor!

Kangaskhan™ — Very nurturing. Loves to take care of babies, pets, and anything that needs love and affection. Loyal and very protective.

Krabby™ — Its name says it all. It's crabby, cranky, a complainer, and a whiner.

Lapras™ — Gentle, good-natured, giving, helpful. Doesn't like conflict. They don't come any nicer than this!

Machop™ — A loyal companion and a patient teacher. It loves to study the martial arts, then pass its knowledge on to others.

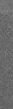

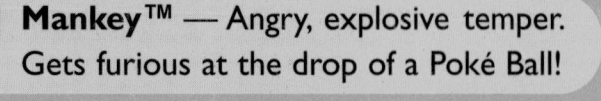

Mankey™ — Angry, explosive temper. Gets furious at the drop of a Poké Ball!

Meowth™ — Devious, ambitious, crafty. Will lie, cheat, and steal to get what it wants. Talks a lot!

Ninetales™ — Vengeful. If you wrong it, it will get back at you, even if it takes 1,000 years!

Pidgeotto™ — Very protective of its possessions and the people and Pokémon it cares about.

Pikachu™ — Can be moody. Takes a while to warm up to new people, but once that happens, is a loyal and trustworthy friend. Tough and determined.

Porygon™ — A real computer whiz! Lives in cyberspace. When it's not on-line, it doesn't exist.

Sandshrew™ — Very picky eater!

Shellder™ — Childish, loves to tease. Will stick its tongue out at you or even spit at you.

Slowpoke™ — Slow-moving and not too bright.

Snorlax™ — Lazy and always hungry. This Pokémon lives only to eat and sleep.

Squirtle™ — Cute and cuddly, but still forceful. A good friend with a good sense of humor. A practical joker.

Tauros™ — Stubborn and hotheaded. It fights first and asks questions later.

Zubat™ — Mostly with Zubat it's take, take, take! It can suck the energy out of the people and Pokémon it comes into contact with, but it also has the potential to be a good friend.

BLAINE'S RIDDLES

BLAINE, THE CINNABAR ISLAND GYM LEADER, ALWAYS TALKS IN RIDDLES. HOW MANY CAN YOU FIGURE OUT?

1 What do Cinnabar Island tourists think is hot . . . and cool?

2 "My gym is right where you put your glasses," Blaine tells Ash. Where is it?

3 If you look at me, you'll see my hands, or at least my face. What am I?

4 Go to the place where firefighters could never win? What place it is?

5 It's not a hat, but it keeps your head dry. If you wear it, it's only because you've already lost it. What is it?

6 Which of Blaine's Pokémon is too hot to handle and can turn all of its opponents into ASH?

7 What do you call any room in a volcano?

8 What do you get if you fill a volcano with ice?

WHO'S THAT POKéMON?

We've zoomed in really close to each of the Pokémon shown below. Can you figure out in each case . . .

WHO'S THAT POKéMON?

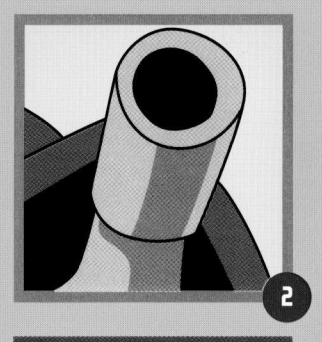

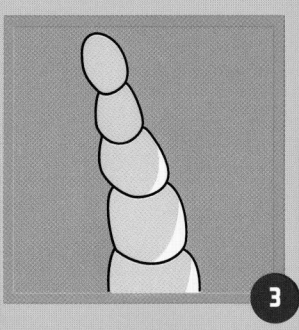

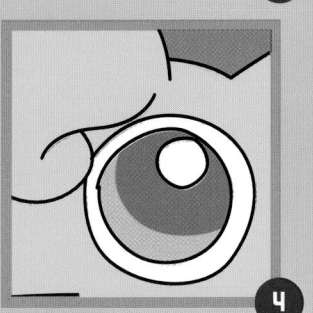

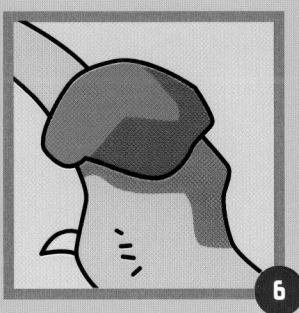

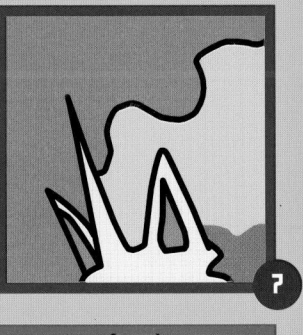

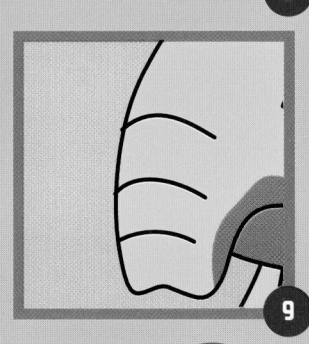

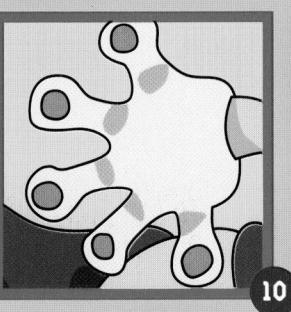

YOU PICK THE WINNER!

Pokémon experts . . . GO! Who will win the following battles? Which Pokémon is stronger when you compare their types? Based on Pokémon type, and assuming that both Pokémon in each battle have the same amount of experience, you pick the winners!

BATTLE #1: SANDSLASH vs. JYNX

The winner is ....

BATTLE #2: WEEZING vs. GLOOM

The winner is ....

BATTLE #3: PIKACHU vs. GOLEM

The winner is ....

BATTLE #4: KADABRA vs. PRIMEAPE

The winner is ....

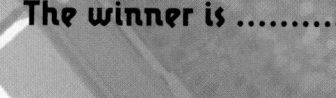

BATTLE #5: SCYTHER vs. CHARIZARD

The winner is ....

BATTLE #6: PIKACHU vs. POLIWRATH

The winner is ....

BATTLE #7: GRAVELER vs. VULPIX

The winner is ....

BATTLE #8: MAGNETON vs. CUBONE

The winner is ....

BATTLE #9: VICTREEBEL vs. PINSIR

The winner is ....

BATTLE #10: HITMONCHAN vs. DODRIO

The winner is ....

CLASSIC POKéMON MATCHES

Whether it's an all-out battle or a contest of skill, Pokémon competitions always mean heart-pumping excitement. Here are some of the most memorable matches of all time!

ASH VS. THE MIKAN ISLAND GYM LEADER CISSY, FOR THE ORANGE ISLAND CORAL-EYE BADGE

This match marked Ash's first face-off with a member of the Orange Crew. It was the first time that Ash had to use his skill as a Pokémon trainer not for a head-to-head battle, but in a contest of Pokémon skill.

The first challenge was to see whose Pokémon could knock over the most cans using a Water Gun Attack. Ash chose Squirtle, Cissy chose Seadra.

"Water Gun, now!" Cissy called.

WHOOSH!

Seadra hit every can, dead center.

But Squirtle was up to the task, as well, and matched Seadra, can for can.

The next challenge was to hit moving targets with the Water Gun Attack. Flying discs were flung into the air. Seadra went first.

SWISH! SWASH! SWOOSH!

Seadra hit target after target. Two targets at a time were fired, then three, and Seadra hit every one.

But once again, Ash's Squirtle matched Seadra, shot for shot. The contest remained deadlocked.

"Next, we'll aim for the same target and see who hits it first," Cissy explained.

"A quick draw contest!" Ash exclaimed. "Cool!"

One, two three . . . DRAW!

Both Squirtle and Seadra hit the target at the same time! Another tie!

Time for a tiebreaker.

"The way we break a tie here on Mikan Island is with a Pokémon Wave Ride," Cissy explained. "The Pokémon have to swim out into ocean, around a flag, and then ride a wave back into shore. All with their trainers riding on their backs!"

"Lapras, I choose you!" Ash called. "Let's win a little swimming race!"

Cissy chose Blastoise.

Ash rode on Lapras, Cissy rode on Blastoise. Out they swam, neck and neck.

Blastoise, the stronger of the two Pokémon, bashed into Lapras. Ash tumbled toward the ocean. Lapras dove in and came up right below Ash, catching him before he plunged into the deep water.

Blastoise took the lead. "See you at the finish line!" Cissy taunted.

Lapras gave Ash an idea. Ash told Lapras to fire an Ice Beam straight to the shore. Then Lapras skidded onto the ice path it had created. Sliding on the ice even faster than it had been swimming, Lapras beat Blastoise back to shore, earning Ash his first Orange Islands badge!

ASH VS. THE NAVEL ISLAND GYM LEADER DANNY, FOR THE ORANGE ISLAND SEA RUBY BADGE

Another contest of skill awaited Ash when he challenged Danny, the Navel Island Gym Leader. If Ash won, he'd earn his second Orange Islands badge and be halfway to the Orange League Tournament.

Before he could even compete head-to-head against Danny and his Pokémon, Ash had to climb up to the very top of a snow-covered mountain — without the help of any Pokémon! Struggling through wind, snow, and ice, Ash finally climbed to the top. Danny was impressed by Ash's determination and challenged him to a Pokémon showdown unlike any other.

The match was made up of three parts. First, the two trainers competed to see whose Pokémon would be the first to freeze a gushing geyser of boiling water.

"I choose you, Nidoqueen!" Danny called, picking a Pokémon with a powerful Ice Attack.

"Ice Attacks, huh?" asked Ash, pulling out a Poké Ball. "In that case, I choose you, Lapras!"

Both trainers called out their attacks at the same moment.

"Ice Beam Attack!" they shouted.

Lapras and Nidoqueen each blasted the rushing water with their arctic breath.

"Come on, Lapras, hang in there!" Ash cried.

"Nidoqueen, Full Power now!" Danny called.

Ash looked on, stunned as Nidoqueen's Ice beam intensified and froze the entire geyser into a solid block of ice.

"It looks like I win the first round," Danny announced. "In the second round we'll compete at sculpting the ice we've created. The first one to carve an ice sled out of his block of ice, using only three Pokémon, wins."

"I choose Pikachu, Bulbasaur, and Charizard!" Ash called.

"And I'm using Machoke, Scyther, and Nidoqueen," Danny announced.

Five of the six Pokémon went right to work, heating, blasting, and chipping away at the blocks of ice. Charizard simply sat, looking away from Ash as if it were bored.

"Come on, Charizard!" Ash cried. "I can't win without you!"

Charizard looked at Ash — then unleashed a furious Flamethrower Attack. When the flames and smoke cleared, Ash's ice sled was done . . . before Danny's.

"Well, I'm not sure exactly how you did it, Ash," Danny said. "But you just won the second round! The final and deciding contest will be a race on our sleds, down the mountain. The first one to reach the beach wins."

Ash and Danny leaped onto their sleds and barreled down the mountain with their Pokémon. Ash bounced and shook as he slid. Bulbasaur tried to steady the sled with its Vine Whip. "Danny didn't tell me the ride would be this rocky!"

Danny took the lead, and was almost at the bottom when Ash flew off a ledge, soared through the air, and crossed the finish line . . . just ahead of Danny!

"You were great, Ash," Danny said. "You chose your Pokémon well, and you won two out of three challenges. For that I give you the Sea Ruby Badge!"

"All right!" Ash shouted. "I couldn't have done it without my Pokémon!"

THE POKéMON BOOK OF WORLD RECORDS

WORLD'S BIGGEST POKéMON

ONIX™
(over 28 feet long)

WORLD'S SMALLEST POKéMON

DIGLETT™
(only 8 inches long)

WORLD'S LIGHTEST POKéMON

GASTLY™ & HAUNTER™
(both weigh only one-fifth of a pound)

WORLD'S HEAVIEST POKéMON

SNORLAX™
(1,014 pounds)

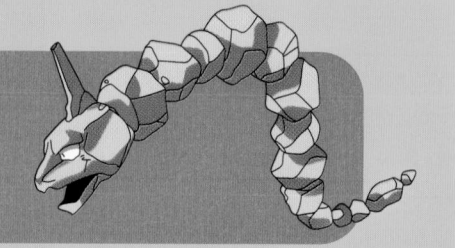

WORLD'S SLOWEST POKéMON

SLOWPOKE™
(hates to move at all)

WORLD'S DUMBEST POKéMON

SLOWPOKE™
(a leader in two catergories, quite an honor)

WORLD'S SMARTEST POKéMON

ALAKAZAM™
(I.Q. of 5,000)

WORLD'S HARDEST POKéMON TO CAPTURE

MEWTWO™
(genetically engineered fighting machine)

WORLD'S MOST UNIQUE POKéMON

EEVEE™
(evolves into three different Pokémon,
depending on which elemental stone is used)

WORLD'S MOST FAMOUS POKéMON

PIKACHU™
(who else?)

TEST YOUR POKé-I.Q.
Are the following statements true or false?

① Dragonite is as smart as a human being.

TRUE ☐   FALSE ☐
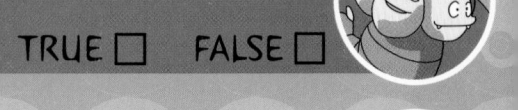

② Vileplume evolves into Gloom only with the Leaf Stone.

TRUE ☐   FALSE ☐

③ Exeggutor has four heads.

TRUE ☐   FALSE ☐

④ At night, Venonat likes to fly near bright lights.

TRUE ☐   FALSE ☐

⑤ Tentacruel's nickname is "the chicken of the sea."

TRUE ☐   FALSE ☐

⑥ There is only one known Togepi in the world.

TRUE ☐   FALSE ☐

⑦ Once Caterpie evolves into Metapod, it becomes a fierce fighter.

TRUE ☐   FALSE ☐

⑧ Dodrio has one head for joy, one head for sorrow, and one head for wisdom.

TRUE ☐   FALSE ☐

⑨ Using its special Rest Technique, Dewgong can bring itself back to full health.

TRUE ☐   FALSE ☐

⑩ Cubone's armor is made from the bones of Pokémon it has defeated in battle.

TRUE ☐   FALSE ☐

⑪ Pokémon researchers knew about Mew from carvings found on cave walls.

TRUE ☐   FALSE ☐

⑫ The female Nidoran's horns are larger than the male's.

TRUE ☐   FALSE ☐

13 Clefairy are found inside Mt. Moon.

TRUE ☐   FALSE ☐

14 Oddish spends all day with its head buried in the ground.

TRUE ☐   FALSE ☐

15 The S.S. *Anne* is a boat docked in Vermilion City.

TRUE ☐   FALSE ☐

16 When Poliwhirl evolves into Poliwrath, the swirl on its stomach changes direction.

TRUE ☐   FALSE ☐

17 Victreebel can be found living on the top of snow-capped mountains.

TRUE ☐   FALSE ☐

18 The fighting Pokémon Hitmonlee and Hitmonchan were named after martial arts film stars Bruce Lee and Jackie Chan.

TRUE ☐   FALSE ☐

19 To get a Kabuto you must first find a Helix Fossil.

TRUE ☐   FALSE ☐

TEAM ROCKET

CHAPTER 12

TEAM ROCKET'S BLASTING OFF AGAIN!

Question: How many members of Team Rocket does it take to screw in a lightbulb?

Answer: Three, but first they have to put on cheesy disguises, invent an overly complicated machine, come up with a dumb plan, then mess the whole thing up!

Never in the history of evildoers has there been a bigger bunch of bunglers than the three main agents of Team Rocket: Jessie, James, and their talking Pokémon, Meowth. They work for the Viridian City Gym Leader and Team Rocket Boss, Giovanni. Their mission is simple — steal rare and valuable Pokémon for their boss. What is never simple is the way they go about doing it.

The Pokémon they are most interested in is none

other than Ash's Pikachu. It has amazing power and determination for such a cute little Pokémon. Again and again, they have trapped Pikachu in electric-proof cages, boxes, bags — you name it. Each time, the resourceful Pokémon has escaped. Other Pikachu-poaching schemes have included protecting themselves by wearing rubber suits, masks, boots, gloves, helmets . . . you get the idea. In each case, Team Rocket ended up shocked out of their shoes (or paws) by searing jolts of Pikachu's powerful Thundershock Attack.

JESSIE AND JAMES

James is the "brains" of Team Rocket, which gives you a clue as to why they always mess up their Pokémon-snatching plans. James is constantly scheming and devising plans that never work out as he had hoped.

These plans often involve all three members of Team Rocket (including Meowth) dressing up in disguises that fool Ash and his friends for about two minutes. After that, everyone sees right through them and realizes that Team Rocket is on the move again.

James's plans also involve complicated machines, with wires, tubes, hoses, and so on. These machines are supposed to do things

like suck up Pokémon using a vacuum, or filter Water Pokémon from a pool, but they always end up backfiring, sending Team Rocket zooming away on a blast of air or a jet stream of water.

Occasionally, James will show a small shred of conscience. Like the time Ash, Misty, and Brock saw Dragonite, the rare Dragon Pokémon, during their visit to a Pokémon researcher in a lighthouse. Team Rocket hid on the cliffs below the lighthouse hoping to capture the unique and mysterious Pokémon, which came floating in on the sea. Jessie fired a rocket that slammed right into Dragonite. The creature roared in pain. At that moment, James doubted that they were doing the right thing, harming such a rare creature.

Jessie, however, put an end to James' attack of conscience by firing another rocket blast right at the retreating Pokémon, who disappeared back into the mists of the sea.

There is no question that Jessie is the more ruthless of the two. There is also no question that Jessie is the leader. She's tough and cunning, bossy and easily enraged. She seems to get as much pleasure in screaming at James as she does in trying to capture Pokémon.

Jessie dreams of fame and fortune, believing that each Team Rocket plot will be the one to please Giovanni and catapult them to superstardom. Still, with such lame plans, disguises, and machines, it seems unlikely that Jessie and James are going to get their hands on Pikachu (or anything else of value) anytime soon!

Jessie's Pokémon: Arbok, Lickitung, Meowth

James's Pokémon: Weezing, Victreebel, Growlithe (stays at home with his family), Meowth

Jessie and James's Motto: Once their useless disguises fail, Jessie and James like to make a big deal about revealing their true identities (as if everybody didn't know already!). This involves the reciting of their motto, which goes like this:

JESSIE and JAMES'S MOTTO

"Prepare for trouble

And make it double!

To protect the world from devastation

To unite all peoples within our nation

To denounce the evils of truth and love!

To extend our reach to the stars above!

Jessie!

James!

Team Rocket! Blast off at the speed of light!

Surrender now or prepare to fight!"

(At this point, Meowth chimes in, saying:)

"'*Meowth!* That's right!'"

MEOWTH

And speaking of Meowth, the Pokémon member of the Team Rocket trio is the only Pokémon who speaks like a human. Meowth, who sounds like a tough guy, is in many ways the smartest of the Team Rocket members.

It's Meowth who usually grabs Pikachu. It's Meowth who pilots the large hot air balloon made in its own image to get

the terrible trio from place to place. And it's often Meowth who points out just how dumb James's latest plan is.

This corrupted cat also has quite a temper and the claws to make it dangerous. More often than not, Jessie and James are the victims of an angry outburst, complete with slashing claws and scratched-up faces. Still, they are Meowth's trainers and the foul feline usually follows their orders.

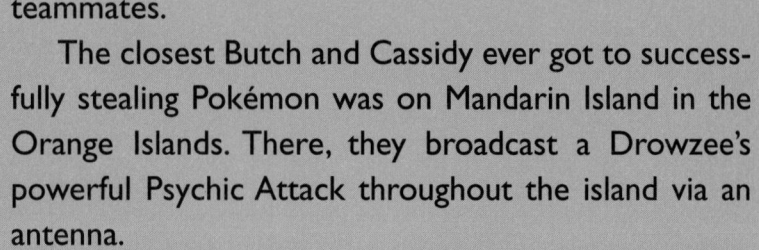

BUTCH AND CASSIDY

Jessie and James aren't the only evil agents working for Giovanni and Team Rocket. Another terrible twosome, Butch and Cassidy — along with their Raticate — also wreak havoc on honest Pokémon trainers. Stealing Pokémon is the name of their game. Fortunately for Ash and his friends (and his Pokémon) they are about as successful as their more famous teammates.

The closest Butch and Cassidy ever got to successfully stealing Pokémon was on Mandarin Island in the Orange Islands. There, they broadcast a Drowzee's powerful Psychic Attack throughout the island via an antenna.

The effect was frightening. Pokémon all around the island stopped obeying their trainers and in some cases even attacked them. Even Ash's Pikachu and Misty's Togepi turned mean and left their trainers to join Butch and Cassidy. Meowth ran away from Jessie

and James to join their Team Rocket rivals. Before Ash managed to stop them, Butch and Cassidy had rounded up a group of Pokémon including Pikachu, Togepi, Poliwhirl, Meowth, Primeape, Vaporeon, Grimer, and Electabuzz, not to mention Jessie's and James's Lickitung, Weezing, Arbok, and Victreebel!

Butch and Cassidy managed to steal all those Pokémon without battling anyone. In fact, they hardly lifted a finger. "Using brute strength to steal Pokémon is so unimaginative," Cassidy said to Jessie and James.

Butch and Cassidy are smarter and more clever than Jessie and James (not much of an achievement if you stop to think about it!). Tormenting and teasing Jessie and James is one of their favorite things to do. When Jessie exclaimed in surprise, "I thought you two were in jail!" Butch informed them that the boss came down to the police station himself and personally bailed them out!

Jessie and James were humiliated. "The boss never does anything like that for us!" Jessie whined.

"That's because we may be on the same team (Rocket, that is), but we are definitely in different leagues," Cassidy shot back in her most insulting tone.

Clearly favored by Giovanni, envied by Jessie and James, and feared by Pokémon trainers everywhere, Butch and Cassidy are an evil force to be reckoned with.

They even rewrote the Team Rocket motto. Here's their version:

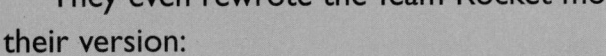

"Prepare for trouble
And make it double!
To infect the world with devastation
To blight all peoples in every nation!
To denounce the goodness of truth
and love!
To extend our wrath to the stars above!
Cassidy!
Butch!
Team Rocket circling Earth all day and night
Surrender to us now or you'll surely lose the fight!"

GIOVANNI

A dark, shadowy figure, Giovanni, the Viridian City Gym Leader and Boss of Team Rocket, sits in his lair pulling the strings like an evil puppet master, petting his purring Persian. Arrogant, greedy, short-tempered, impatient, ruthless, and dangerous (and those are his good qualities!), Giovanni sits at the center of an evil operation that threatens honest Pokémon trainers everywhere!

TEAM ROCKET'S BIGGEST BLUNDERS, STUPIDEST SCHEMES, DOPIEST DISGUISES, AND MOST PATHETIC PLOTS!

• Dressing up in ballet tutus to try to steal the Water Pokémon at the Cerulean City Gym, during the Sensational Cerulean Sister's underwater ballet.

• Dressing up as TV news reporters (including Meowth in a mustache) to try to steal Pokémon at the opening round of the Pokémon League Tournament on the Indigo Plateau.

• Setting up a snack stand and selling cookies outside the

Cinnabar Island Gym. They got no customers and no Pokémon.

• Pretending to be magicians during Kids Day, so they could make Pikachu disappear. The kids saw right through their scheme, and so did Ash!

• Flying Ash, Misty, Brock, and Pikachu in a blimp to the Orange Islands, to try to steal Pikachu. Naturally, the blimp crashed and Pikachu got away.

• Climbing all the way up a huge mountain carrying full back-packs, then tossing a boulder down toward Ash and a group of Pokémon research scientists. The boulder was flung back up by a pair of Machoke and, of course, landed right on Team Rocket.

• Digging a hole to catch Pokémon, then falling into the hole themselves — again and again and again!

• Dressing up like pirates to steal a troupe of performing Pokémon on a showboat. The performers combined their powers to easily defeat Team Rocket.

• Scooping up what they thought was a large number of Water Pokémon in a big net, only to discover that all they got was a Tentacruel and a Psyduck. As if that wasn't bad enough, they were then stopped by a Golduck.

• Coming to the Orange Islands to steal Pokémon in a fake Magikarp submarine. A real Magikarp was attracted to their ship, then learned it was a fake, evolved into Gyarados, and sent Team Rocket blasting off again!

NEW POKéMON

CHAPTER 13

HERE COME THE NEW POKéMON!

You've been training for a while now and you've caught them all, right? Wrong!

Just when you thought you had all the Pokémon there are, here come 100 new ones! That's right! One hundred brand-new Pokémon from the Silver and Gold games.

Who are they? What do they do? Are they like the Pokémon we know and love? Here's a sneak peek:

• The new Pokémon will live in some new places that we haven't even seen yet.

• Some will use brand-new, never-before-seen attacks.

• You'll have to wait for Pokémon to wake up before battling with them.

• And here's the coolest tidbit of all — some of the new Pokémon will be evolutions and pre-evolutions of current Pokémon! That means that some of the original 150 Pokémon that you thought could never evolve now will. Others of the new 100 Pokémon are pre-evolutions, or younger versions of some of the original 150. Stay tuned for details!

Between the television show and the first Pokémon movie, you've already met a few of these new 100. Here's the scoop on them:

TOGEPI

Togepi was hatched from a rare Pokémon egg that Ash found during a fossil dig in Grandpa Canyon. There is only one known Togepi in the whole world. Misty was the first person Togepi saw right after it hatched, so Togepi thinks that Misty is its mother. Now Togepi won't let anyone else be its trainer. But that's okay with Misty. She's crazy about her Togepi, and gives it the extra love and attention this baby Pokémon needs. Misty thinks that Togepi may have the ability to teleport itself and others from place to by moving its tiny arms back and forth. Only time will tell.

MARILL

Marill is a Water Pokémon. It's sweet-natured, lovable, cute, and very talented. Its large round ears are so sensitive, they can detect sounds at great distances. And Marill's great hearing teams up perfectly with Venonat's radar ability to search for hidden, lost, or distant Pokémon.

Marill is also an excellent swimmer. The ball on its tail floats in the water, helping Marill to swim in rough seas, and showing its trainer where it is at all times.

Marill gets along well with Togepi, who loves to hang onto Marill's tail and play with it like a toy.

SNUBBULL

Snubbull is a fairy Pokémon. Although it has a mean-looking face, Snubbull is usually very sweet. Snubbull also will brag if it thinks it can beat an opponent.

PUZZLE ANSWERS

Answers to Blaine's Riddles

1) Hot springs. They are really hot, steamy baths, but they feel so good, tourists think they're cool!

2) "It's right in front of your eyes." Ash was standing right in front of the gym.

3) A clock

4) The inside of a volcano

5) A wig you wear if you've already lost your hair

6) Magmar

7) A Lava-tory

8) A snow cone

Answers to Who's That Pokémon

1) Venusaur	6) Alakazam
2) Blastoise	7) Rapidash
3) Ekans	8) Dewgong
4) Jigglypuff	9) Drowzee
5) Primeape	10) Mr. Mime

You Pick the Winner! Answers

Battle #1: Jynx. Ice-Type Pokémon have the advantage over Ground Types.

Battle #2: Weezing. Poison-Type Pokémon have the advantage over Grass Types.

Battle #3: Pikachu. Water-Type Pokémon have the advantage over Rock Types.

Battle #4: Kadabra. Psychic-Type Pokémon have the advantage over Fighting Types.

Battle #5: Charizard. Fire-Type Pokémon have the advantage over Bug Types.

Battle #6: Pikachu. Electric-Type Pokémon have the advantage over Water Types.

Battle #7: Graveler. Rock-Type Pokémon have the advantage over Fire Types.

Battle #8: Cubone. Ground-Type Pokémon have the advantage over Electric Types.

Battle #9: Pinsir. Bug-Type Pokémon have the advantage over Grass Types.

Battle #10: Hitmonchan. Fighting-Type Pokémon have the advantage over Normal Types.

True or False Answers

1) True

2) False. Vileplume doesn't evolve into Gloom. Gloom evolves into Vileplume (using the Leaf Stone).

3) False. Exeggutor has three heads.

4) True

5) False. Tentacruel's nickname is "the gangster of the sea."

6) True

7) False. Metapod doesn't move.

8) False. The third head is for anger.

9) True

10) False. Cubone's armor is made from the bones of ancient Pokémon.

11) True

12) False

13) True

14) True

15) False. The name of the boat is the S.S. *Anne*.

16) False. The swirl changes direction when Poliwag evolves into Poliwhirl.

17) False. Victreebel lives deep in the jungle.

18) True

19) False. You must find a Dome Fossil.

POKÉMON®

Gotta catch 'em all!™

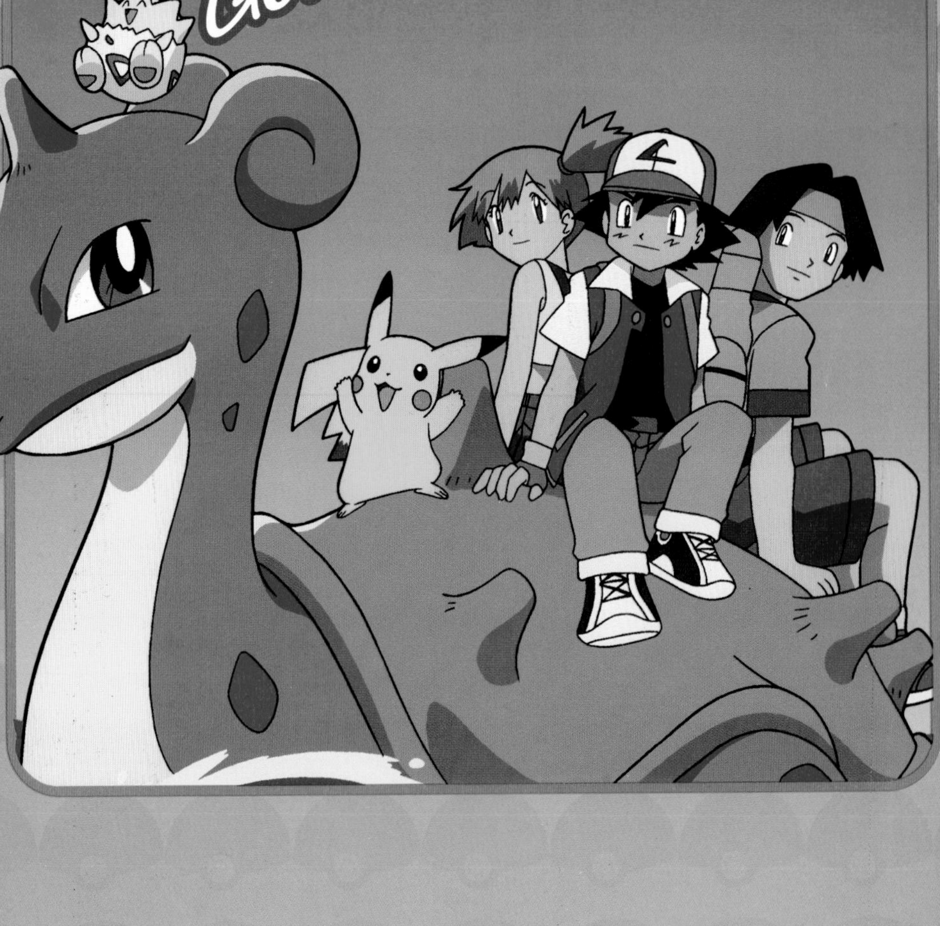